The Human War

PTSD Recovery Guide for Returning Soldiers

Douglas H. Ruben, Ph.D.

Outskirts Press, Inc.
Denver, Colorado

Healthy men and women across the sea,
Fighting bravely for a country tis of thee,
Proudly showing energy,
For a mighty cause for all to see,
Just how brilliant the armed forces can be.

To my lovely wife,

Arlene

Deployment

The Human War - PTSD recovery guide for returning soldiers

Douglas H. Ruben, Ph. D

Number of copies - 1

PLEASE PRINT CLEARLY		
Date Out	Phone #	Borrower's Name LAST, FIRST

This book must be returned after 30 days.
Replacement cost will be invoiced if book is not returned.

Vous devez retourner ce livre après 30 jours.
Le coût de remplacement sera facturé si le
livre n'est pas retourné.

RETURN BY/DATE DE RETOUR		

Contents

For Starters, What is PTSD?

Life traumas are tragic enough. But enduring the difficulty of war adds unbelievable stress to proud people serving the country. Not just soldiers, but for their families back home. Leaving home is only half the battle. Abroad the soldier faces new surroundings, new routines, and must adjust rapidly under pressure of fear and enemy attacks. All of that takes courage. Sometimes that courage is lost during battles, sometimes after battles. Victory feels good, but the shock of combat, and of coming home, can hurt. It hurts big. Courage tested sometimes weakens when you come home.

But there is a way to prevent this weakness. Prevent weakness by learning, memorizing, and applying the steps of personal power that revive courage. It keeps your mind alert, your confidence high, and your spirit soaring. This recovery guide does that. It tells you the exact steps to take to prevent moments of weakness. These are steps that stay with you long after your tour of duty ends. Read over this recovery guide anytime you need a dose of pride. Let these steps be your emergency kit to restoring faith in yourself and your country.

The Road to Recovery

Ending stress is the greatest feeling in the world. Your stressors probably involved captivity or constant threat of attack. Whether your captivity was friendly or torturous, liberating from captivity stopped that paralyzing feeling of doom. Hostage negotiators acutely know, for example, that hostages were prone to overreact if they feel helpless. They may be rebellious. Or, they may be submissive. Rebellious ones risk endangering their lives and lives of other hostages. Submissive ones suffer demoralizing emotional pain and may be manipulated at the whim of crazed gunmen.

But what happens when a hostage is freed? What happens when some war-trauma experience is over? Do you feel anything? Are you numb? Do sensations peak of fear, anger, and need for revenge? Do you feel a consuming need to learn everything about you abductors?

Perhaps so. This chapter will tell you why you feel this way and the rest of the book will tell you what you can do about it.

Anger, Fear, Loss and Trauma

Anger usually is behind this hunger for knowledge. You aggressively seek information on your abductors as an expression of outrage. The more intensively you immerse yourself deep into the stacks of literature, the more control you feel over anger. Defused anger allows you to return to your duty, jobs, and eventually family and life routines.

But while anger has an outlet, fear may not. The most severe impact of being a prisoner or suffering horrible trauma is *toxic fear*. Toxic fear is when your mind and body undergo a "shock to the system" causing complete breakdown of your senses and feeling immobilized. You can't think, you can't act, you can't do anything. Trauma is profoundly overwhelming. You feel disoriented, stunned, in a daze of disbelief, and cannot even mentally remember events that just took place. Over the next few days and months you can't sleep; can't eat; can't see friends; can't think straight; and feel waves of chills rushing through your body. Noises, light rays, even darkness instantly trigger rapid heart-beating and sweaty palms. Muscles tighten, your breathing gets tougher, and you honestly believe you're going to faint.

You are not crazy; you are suffering effects of *Post-Traumatic Syndrome* (PTSD). These also include recurrent nightmares, flashbacks, sudden irritability, and odd changes in your personality. Instead of being an extrovert, you become an introvert. Instead of a passive-submissive caretaker, you become a belligerently aggressive cynic. Opposite shifts in personality occur without you realizing it and may look odd to people around you. But don't despair; they still love you dearly and are confident you can pull out of it.

The symptoms of PTSD may initially seem to be part of a normal response to an overwhelming experience. Only if those symptoms persist beyond three months do we speak of them being part of a disorder. Sometimes the disorder surfaces months or even years later. In all, there are three ways to talk about the symptoms. These include *intrusive symptoms, avoidant symptoms, and symptoms of hyper-arousal.*

Intrusive Symptoms

Returning soldiers suffer from a type of PTSD where the traumatic event "intrudes" on their current lives. This can happen in sudden, vivid memories that are accompanied by painful emotions. Sometimes the trauma is "re-experienced." This is called a flashback. Flashbacks are recollections that are so strong that the individual thinks he or she is actually experiencing the trauma again or seeing it unfold before his or her eyes.

At times, the re-experienced sensation occurs in nightmares. In PTSD adults, distressing dreams of the traumatic event may evolve into generalized nightmares of monsters, of rescuing others or of threats to self or others. At times, the re-experience comes as a sudden, painful onslaught of emotions that seem to have no cause. These emotions are often of grief that brings tears, fear or anger. Victims say these emotional experiences occur repeatedly, much like memories or dreams about the traumatic event.

it. That's the scary part. Post-trauma sufferers who suspect they got zapped by some wartime experience may feel helpless and hopeless. Awareness of the trauma may bring back graphically disturbing memories or sensations of helplessness. Like a virtual-reality experience, you may have catapulted into re-living tragedy as if as if it was happening all over again.

Who would do that? In theory, nobody. But ugly symptoms do not magically dissipate in time. They are not like a cold or flu virus running it natural course in the body until symptoms vanish. Trauma not only recedes deeply in your thoughts, it is "systemic." That means, it is like a cancer. Deeply rooted fears spread to everything you do in your life and become interwoven in the your daily fabric. You can protest the trauma and say, "I hate this and won't suffer it anymore." But that does nothing. Once in you, trauma stubbornly persists until you directly confront it with self-control techniques.

So, let's confront them now. If you don't know what your fears are, hypnosis or talking aloud with caring others is your first step. Then, consider the many techniques offered throughout this guidebook. Nearly ever step listed here is at your fingertips. The last step (Step 11), introduces methods for PTSD-removal with the guidance of a counselor.

How to Spot Trouble

See you if you can answer these questions as either "yes" or "no."

1. Are you doing too many things?
2. Are you doing enough?
3. Are you avoiding or escaping problems?
4. Are you afraid all of the time?
5. Do you feel rushed all of the time?
6. Are you angry all of the time?
7. Do you take everything personally?
8. Do you think nobody cares?
9. Are you getting enough sleep?
10. Are you feeling out of control?
11. Are you getting bored?
12. Are you afraid of not making it?
13. Are you having many physical problems?
14. Do you have bad nightmares?
15. Do you get flashbacks?
16. Do you hate being alone?
17. Do you distrust everybody?

18. Do you startle easily?
19. Do you feel numbness, and lack emotion?
20. Do you always like taking revenge?

These questions ask if personal symptoms are out of control. The questions you answered "yes" to are problem areas, whereas the "no" answers can be left alone. With this self-screening of symptoms, proceed onto the next chapter to begin repairing your life.

Focus: Thoughts and Actions

The following list compiles the fastest and easiest ways to interrupt wrong thinking and the upset emotions that ruin healthy civilian living.

1. Slow down your thinking.
2. Slow down your actions.
3. Try not to request so much attention from others.
4. Stick with one topic, finish it, then go to another one.
5. No time for grudges; let them pass.
6. Try it again, Trial and error are okay.
7. Follow through. If you say it, do it.
8. Can't do it? Okay, ask for help.
9. Stick with the facts—only deal with what you know, not what you think is happening. Ask questions.
10. Upset somebody? Apologize. Forget being right.
11. Somebody upset you? Tell it to the person. Say, "It's no big deal." Let it slide.
12. Be a good listener. Hear it all.
13. Feel embarrassed? It's okay, so does everyone else.

14. Stick with today, what's happening right now. Worry about tomorrow another day.

15. Situations remind you of a bad situation? Look around. Find out how it's different. It's not the same.

16. Expecting the worst? Find something positive about the situation. Turn negative thinking into positive thinking.

Back into the Routine

Here are rapid strategies to re-align your daily routines, habits, and adjustment to a civilian schedule.

1. Know your routine. You don't have one? Invent one. Everyday, the same thing.
2. Working? Good. If not, find a job. Busy means you're not rehashing. Even great stories wear thin after awhile.
3. Talk about the things that did happen, not things invented. Keep the made-up stuff to yourself.
4. Hard to concentrate? Look around you. Find things you can count. Things you can predict. Simple things. Number of desks in office. Number of phone calls you make. The simpler, the better.
5. Feel wired? Breathe slowly in and out.
6. Get people to say you look calm. And look calm.
7. Thoughts feed anger. Say to yourself, "So what, it's no big deal."
8. Angry? Count 10 seconds, breathe slowly in and out. Sit down. Talk slowly, not fast.

9. Do things that make you wait. Wait in line. Be the last one. It's okay. There's no rush anyway.
10. Forgetful? It happens. Write notes. Ask people to remind you. Check off the item when you do it.
11. Waking up too early? Stay in bed. Remove the covers. Loosen clothes. Feel the chill. Describe things in your bedroom. When tired, turn on your side and put covers back on.
12. Staying up too late? You're used to guard duty. Go to bed earlier. Stay in bed. No eating, reading, or watching TV before bed. Just hit the covers.

Fight Fear with Courage

Here are ways to conquer anxiety, fear, and internal insecurity. Use the talent of your courage—the power of your military training—to recover from sad or slow days, from internally feeling defeated.

1. Hang around other people. Talk to them. Topic can be anything. Just blend in .
2. Stay in situations. Let people know you'll stay in situations. Talk about doing it.
3. Feel tears coming? So cry. Proud people cry, too.
4. Try new things. You don't have to know how to do them. Once you got it, show another how it's done.
5. Take a risk. A small one at first. Take another risk. A little larger one. Don't jump too quick. Do what you can do.
6. It's okay to brag—when you're afraid. Talk about what you're great at. It's the truth. And that's when you need to know it.

7. Lead others in songs, prayer, or work. Never done it before? Nobody else has either.

8. Tough sleep? Close eyes, tighten and loosen muscles. Breathe slowly in and out. Think of home.

9. Think why you are lucky, not out of luck.

10. Try, honestly, to see things as a challenge.

11. Forget competition. You don't have to be better. You just have to do things. Jus t know you're good, real good.

12. Figure out what scares you. Deal with it straight on. Breath slowly in and out.

13. Say "Whom Am I?" Look in the mirror. Remember who you were in combat or active duty. Now make that person in the mirror better.

14. Don't be the person you once were. Forget it. Once was enough. Now you're better.

15. Noises bother you? Tell yourself what they are. Not what you think they are .

16. Senses real alert? It's common. You feel like you have eyes in the back of your head. Look straight forward. Deal with what you see. Deal with what you're doing. Stay on-task.,

17. Want to get away? Turn around. Go back the other direction. Stay there. Now, stay there longer.

18. When afraid of people, seek them out. Talk. Say things even if you think you're dumb.

19. No drinking or using drugs for escape. If you can face bullets, you can face fear.

Fight Failure with Courage

Courage is your integrity. It is your underlying force. Inside of you lies this seismic force of bravery that you forgot. It's there, awaiting retrieval against the most sinister enemy you've faced. That enemy is failure. Below are quick, efficient strategies to protect yourself from losing confidence over fleeting or obsessive thoughts of failure.

1. Things not going right? You're home now. Let it take time.
2. Do it right, but mistakes are normal.
3. Tell people it's okay for you to make mistakes.
4. Laugh about your mistakes.
5. Looking stupid is part of learning. Let it happen.
6. Compliment people. For anything—not just great stuff.
7. Accept compliments.
8. Tell somebody you're scared. You're not bothering them. Tell them, then let it pass.
9. After you say things, forget re-playing it over in your head. It's done. Over.

10. After you do things, forget how it could have been better. There's always a next time. Let it pass.
11. Think you look funny? Maybe stupid? So what? Everybody else does at one point or another.
12. People say you've changed. You have. It's for the better.
13. Sex a problem? You want to have sex but can't? Go slower. Rebuild. Never get angry at what you can't do. Enjoy what you can do each time you have sex.
14. Scary dreams? Even victories can't stop dreams. Talk about them. Talk about why you're brave in our dreams.
15. Feel guilty you made it, but another didn't? That person died for freedom. You would, too. You're alive to keep freedom alive.
16. Bad luck? It's not luck. It's your expectations. Lower them. Start realistically. Do things you can do.

Fight Pain with Courage

Before war, you had no pain. In war, you felt invincible. From war, you got wounded either physically or emotionally, in ways nobody can understand or even imagine. Your pain is real, hurtful, and has changed the course of your life. But that new course can be good, beneficial, and not a scar of disaster for your life. Below are ways people with PTSD pain fight back against unbearable pain.

1. Forget worries. It hurts worse to think about your pain and how it limits you.
2. Pain goes away when you keep busy.
3. We're all disabled in some way.
4. It hurts? Focus on parts of your body that do not hurt.
5. It hurts? Focus on what people tell you. Not on what you're telling yourself.
6. Do things as normally as you can. One steps at a time.
7. Slow down. Take slow breaths. Breathe in and out. Talk to yourself about what you're doing right.

8. People look at you funny? You don't owe them explanations. Just keep moving. One day they'll undestand.

9. Hate doing things in a wheelchair? Look at it like clothing. You wear it when you get up in the morning. You take it off when you go to bed.

10. Pain prevents sex? Ask yourself, how many different ways are there to have sex. Be creative.

11. Pain makes you angry? Count to ten before you blame somebody. They didn't do it.

12. Feel less human? Wrong. You're superhuman. You went through things most people can't even imagine, and survived.

Fight Stress with Courage

Do you get upset, worried, feel nervous? Eliminate this stress by changing your priorities. You are first. You have the gusto, chivalry, and incredible intelligence to resist temptations of fear and stress in life. Below are the strategies brave people use who refuse to fall apart and know, inside, they are resilient.

1. Always sleep at night. Lack of sleep makes you anxious.
2. Always eat. Even if you're not hungry, eat a little. Do this for one to two months, after stress.
3. Excitement of your arrival lasts today, maybe tomorrow, not for a month.
4. Catch a cold? You're not down in the dumps. Don't feel depressed. It's the first time your body slowed down. Now you get sick like everybody else.
5. Talking fast. Moving fast? Slow down. Blend into the crowd. You don't have to prove your special. You are special. People will know it by looking at you.
6. Feel like it's not over? You're right. Maybe it's not. But it is for now. You're home.

7. Can't organize your time? Most people can't. Look over your priorities. Break them down into tiny parts. Do them in order. No rush.
8. Hate everything around you? Even loved ones? Talk it out. Tell a counselor, clergy, or best friend. Let go of it or you'll hate yourself next.
9. Balance your habits. Not too much of anything

For Returning Vets

Now you are home. You made it. You endured the long tours of duty. You exceeded your own and your immediate commander's expectations of physical and emotional stamina under constant threats of death and uncertainty. Every car, every civilian, every street, every market you traveled through, who knows what might happen. Would you get through it alive? Would tomorrow come? Well, it did. You're safe and at home. You're in a place stranger than the foreign country you were in. Your own house. Or, maybe the house you grew up in. A home reminiscent of positive times, no matter how long ago these good times were. How can you restore the good times? How can you re-enter the civilian world you once lived in? Below are strategies for blending into this new reality, and dodging some common mistakes.

1. Celebrate. Pat yourself on the back. Tell yourself you did a great job. You did.
2. Talk to Vets.
3. Home is strange. Don't expect to pick up where you left off.

4. People care. They really do. Even if you can't see it.
5. Pretend you're Rip Van Winkle. Away for a long time. Even if it 's been a short time.
6. You'll see things your family won't see. You've been away. Things look differently.
7. You'll feel things your family won't feel. Like a stranger. That's normal. You're used to war, not a home.
8. Bored a lot? Again, this is normal. You were busy. You were on alert. Now you're off duty. Less tension.
9. Feel rejected? Forget it. Even loved ones aren't sure how to greet you. It can be awkward.
10. Being stared at? It happens. You're a celebrity. Enjoy the attention.
11. Lots of stories to tell. Not everybody wants to hear them. That's okay. Remember how you hate to sit through family slide shows? Bingo. It's the same thing.
12. Work is calling. Go for it.
13. Never forget. You don't have to.
14. Anti-war people say you're bad. So what. That's one opinion.
15. Angry? Don't hold it in. You're not alone. There's plenty out there like yourself. Seek help.
16. Visit your doctor. Get a checkup.
17. Visit a counselor. Just one visit. Walk through any and all anxieties. Don't wait. Don't be overly confident. Just be natural.
18. Vets of other wars don't see it like you do. That's okay. They fought different wars. There's no right and wrong experience. To each his own.
19. Your spouse or special friend is passionate. So are you. Enjoy it. Enjoy some more. Then let it return to normal.
20. When the party's over, it doesn't mean you're not important anymore. Just ask your family, they'll tell you. You are important.

How to Control Your Anger At Home

"Control your anger!" Ever hear someone say that to you? Probably. And you hated it. Anybody would. Nobody likes to be criticized and especially hearing that you are out of control. But let's face it. Calming down in war or non-war situations is hard to do. When things aren't going right, you get upset, and possibly lose your cool. Losing your cool around family after you return home is even tougher.

Fact is, it is impossible to be perfectly composed over every mishap in the household. Nobody can just "turn the other cheek" and pretend the antique dish didn't break, or pretend the milk really didn't spill all over your cell-phone. Forget it. These things really happen. And the sooner reality hits you, the stronger you are against your anger.

That is why you want to read this chapter. It talks about what actually makes you angry at yourself and family members. Parts of anger called "urges" are laid out for you to spot, stop, and surrender before body tension escalates into raging aggression. First, let's get an idea of what causes an urge, and then spend the rest of the chapter focusing on simple ways to control your urge of anger.

What is an Urge?

Urges are stressful periods of life usually lasting a short while but hectic to deal with. Urges can be a powerful drive to want something, or get away from something, or make something happen. Motivation to speak, act or react is strong or *urgent.* Urges are not automatic. They are caused by six things that happen at any given moment. These include:

1. **You are under a time limit.**
2. **You want something.**
3. **There are no alternatives to choose from.**
4. **You have two or more things you want to do simultaneously.**
5. **You have obstacles in the way of doing something.**
6. **In the past you had bad experiences with situations like these.**

Let's consider these closer.

1. You are under a time limit.

Rushing around a busy household and balancing the juggling act of kids, office and leisure can be a mess. Routines get interrupted, delayed or modified. Something always goes wrong. No matter how early you awoke that morning, or told the kids time and again to be ready for school, it always happens. They forget. You forget. And the best laid plans of mice and men evaporate into thin air.

The balancing act gets more difficult when there is a time pressure. You *must* get to work on time. Kids *must* be outside for the school bus. You *must* get to the doctor's appointment by the hour. And the list abounds with countless reasons that time suddenly becomes a scarce commodity. When this happens, limits on time spoil patience. Time deadlines mobilize you into a frenzy of actions, from speeding up your pace to forcing others around you to rush. Perhaps you can do it. But generally kids cannot. The faster they go, the more mistakes they make; they more confused they get; the more tired they feel; and the more angrier they become.

2. You want something.

You want it when? Now! Urges can't wait. Urges range from biological urges such as hunger or thirst or sex, to personal needs such as watching TV. At times the desire for needs is higher than other times. Under physical pain or fatigue, lying down to take a nap is highly desirable. Hunger from missing breakfast and lunch causes intense cravings for food. Or maybe the situation dictates immediate action. A fly is still on the wall and in perfect target range for the fly swatter, but it must be hit within seconds or else it flies away. Or that pesky mosquito swarming around your face; smack it now before it bites you.

Satisfying your urges may be important, but it may compromise your family's needs and interfere with logic. Take, for example, when Jacob, Andy's father, stopped in the middle of helping Andy with his homework to catch a mosquito. Naturally mosquitoes pose *some* danger to his son, but *not that much danger*. Jacob climbed up on top of a weakly supported chair to block the mosquito in its path and made futile swats that put spots on the wall. Jacob's *compulsive* need to end that mosquito's life shows he lacked urge control. Jacob could not wait until later to kill the mosquito, or at least until after helping Andy with his homework. The faster urges are acted upon, the more aggressively explosive an adult's behavior will appear.

3. There are no alternatives to choose from.

Urges also arise when you don't know what to do. You face a mountain of problems all pointing in no direction. And you cannot figure out how to satisfy the urge. No good solution comes to mind. Making sandwiches seem simple enough, for instance, but what if there is no bread, no meat, no cheese, and no mustard. Frustration rises little by little, propelling into agitation. Once agitation reaches a blasting point, outwardly your anger may look bizarre, random, or even out of touch with reality.

4. You have two or more things you want to do simultaneously.

Plans always backfire to some extent. But it is worse when you need to do two or more things simultaneously. No doubt you are one of those talented, multi-tasked people who thrive on being busy. Most people can do two to three tasks simultaneously, usually talking on cell-phone while surfing the net, while eating. Concentration remains strong, and you juggle the tasks perfectly— until you're interrupted. Interruptions of one task is bad, but interrupting two, three or ongoing tasks is pure Hell. You'll get impatient, angry, sarcastic, blame others for ruining your concentration. You may even abort the two or three tasks you're working on.

5. You have obstacles in the way of doing something.

Many situations arise when you know exactly what you want to do but cannot do it because of obstacles. Think of road rage. Driving to work this morning, you estimated correct travel time until you saw the terrible traffic from road construction. Construction that started early that morning and you knew nothing about. It delays you from work, ruins your time schedule, and is infuriating. You are stuck; a victim trapped by unplanned roadblocks that threaten your goals. Obstacles in the way of your life may sabotage plans but they also eat away at patience around the family.

6. In the past you had bad experiences with situations like these.

Not every situation is bad. In fact, even unpleasant events in your history improve through years of experience. However, there are situations that stay the same no matter how many different ways you try to improve the situation. Even when you reassure yourself with, "c'mon, it's not that bad," it still feels awful. And, truth is, it really is that bad. It's bad because you had a nasty encounter with certain people, objects or events associated with the situation. While abroad on duty, for example, you remembered the pale evening sky and chilly air after a balmy day. You remember how thirsty you always got in the evening, no matter how hydrated you stayed during the day. Now, at home, warm days turn to colder evenings, and suddenly it's déjà vu. You feel impatiently thirsty and an impulse away from drinking everything in sight.

These five conditions make urges occur. Surprisingly, most people are unaware urges strike when they are feeling stressful or off guard. Or, that urges always follow a predictable pattern from start to finish.

Pattern of Urges

Urges go through very distinct steps as they slowly worsen and you feel out of control. Lack of control is nothing to be proud of but neither should you be ashamed of uncontrolled urges. Everybody experiences them. Watch out for urges as they rise in three steps: Threshold, Peak and Calm.

Threshold. Urges intensify more and more as time passes. At first a basic need, craving, or desire to do something remains harmless. Two minutes later that same harmless urge is eating away like a cancer at your conscious. Why is this?

The threshold stage describes a period when two predictable changes happen inside of you that are not visible to other people. Quickly, as if catapulted by a cannon, you feel physical changes, followed by changes in thinking. Physical changes appear in the autonomic or involuntary nervous system that control respiration, circulation, digestion, glands and other reflexes. Sudden increases occur in heart-beat, pulse rate, swallowing, blinking, sweating, and muscle contractions around the stomach, chest, shoulder and neck. Muscle tension also feels like a "butterfly taking flight" in your stomach mixed with flush sensations rushing up and down your spine. Face color may change, and hands become wet with perspiration. Your stimulated nervous system discharges a rush of adrenalin creating more and more discomfort.

Physical arousal is similar to food, alcohol or drug withdrawal. At first slowly building tensions elevate to desperate needs. You feel your body aching for the thing, object or event you want and delaying its attainment shortens your patience. Five to ten minutes into an urge episode the autonomic effects may worsen to watery eyes, stomach cramps, pacing, and need for urination.

Right in the heat of autonomic arousal, your thoughts spring forth with ideas that *something is very wrong.* Muscular stiffness pair with your insides doing acrobatics. This sensation *will automatically trigger thoughts about doom, anger and blame.* You can't control vicious thoughts regarding why you *must* do the thing you want and *why it has no business being delayed.* Thoughts blurt out to you in obsessive echoes and so loud in your thoughts, you'd think everybody standing near you could hear it. But not so; only you hear the thoughts. Bursting thoughts usually take one of these themes:

1. Where is the thing?
2. Why isn't it here now?
3. What's wrong with the person who was supposed to bring it to me?
4. Things like this always happen to me!
5. This delay is inexcusable!

Thinking is obsessive. You criticize yourself for *being so stupid,* or blame another person for denying you of the need you want. Hank waited and waited for his son to finish in the bathroom. Eight-year old Billy just didn't move that quickly. The drive to school took 10 minutes and school started in 15 minutes, leaving little leeway time in between.

Angry thoughts deflect attention from the real situation and toward scapegoated family members. For example, you may yell at your child for the smallest infraction. Your child cannot understand what he did wrong. Take Billy, for example. Like most children, Billy scares easily. He trembles and stiffens at the shrieking voice of his your anger, believing that he is bad or has somehow disappointed you. He is *ashamed.* In other words, one deadly result of uncontrolled urges at the threshold stage is imposing guilt on family members. Guilt instantly makes them afraid, reluctant, and passive.

Peak. This stage marks the natural turning point of urges. As time increases, intensity of urges also increases, reaching the peak at the very top.

Now you're anger is really rolling. By the peak stage, autonomic arousal is fully in motion; muscle twitches and tightness are harder to hide. Visible anger dominates your entire body even if you are generally a mild–mannered person. Friends and family looking at

28

you might even ask if you are okay or suffering an illness. They're not accustomed to seeing this behavior in you—nor are you. Behaviors you display shift from anger to sadness to manic and bizarre explosions of frustration. Mood swings also are heavily verbal and physical. You swear, become defensive, and yell.

Your temper flares and it looks "childish." By the time anger defuses and the wave passes, damage done to all who watched you is unforgivable and largely irreversible.

The Calm after the Storm. Scientifically, urges pass through both threshold and peak before they subside. Twenty to thirty minutes after urges first start, with no relief still in sight, you take on a new attitude about the urge; "oh well." You surrender to the urge and realize you cannot get what you want. Surrender, however, is not always a passive experience. There are two ways you might resign to emotional surrender. First is to openly resist failure, and the second is blaming yourself or your family member for rudely denying you of what you wanted. Let's consider these more closely.

Two Wrong Ways that adults react when urges fade

1. **Admit failure and not seek new alternatives.**
2. **Resist failure and blame yourself or another family member.**

Admit failure and not seek new alternatives. You didn't get what you wanted or it took so long to get it, that it really doesn't matter anymore. You stop your anger, stop your yelling, and figure the nirvana you seek is not found. Now you turn try to solve the problem again. But this time, you face the *basic problem.* How can I get what I want? Marcus really wanted to pick up a few groceries at lunch before returning to work. Except, he also had to shuttle his daughter Sally from elementary school to her dance lesson starting at 1:00. By the time Marcus snuck out of the office and made it to his car, less than a half hour was left to rush to the groceries and transport Sally. Marcus arrived at Sally's school in minutes. Then proceeded to the grocery store. *Forget it!* Traffic was so congested to pull off this second task. No matter how blatantly upset Marcus was toward other motorists for *being so stupid on the road,* time passed too quickly. He simply couldn't go to both places. He ran out of time.

Marcus surrendered to time constraints and his anger vanished. But not before Marcus mishandled his anger and blew off some steam. Anger is gone; no apologies, no solutions found. It just dies. And supposedly, everybody who suffered through the ordeal just forgets about it.

2. Resist Failure and Blame Yourself or another family member. The scenario could have been different. What if Marcus didn't let go of the anger? What if he took it out on himself or his daughter? Marcus' unmet urge might disappear to passage of time, but his anger about not satisfying the urge lingers on. His distorted thinking becomes accusatory; he stews over why he *should have been able to do it,* and that his mistakes were *preventable.* Anguish over mistakes triggers fierce self–criticism. Marcus becomes judge and jury. He finds himself *guilty, stupid and sloppy* for not satisfying his urges.

Guilt-blaming is a bad model in front of a child. For example, impressionable Sally heard her father rant and rave over a mistake. This perplexes Sally. Sally innocently wonders "Why is he angry?" It doesn't make sense? Why is he upset over small, insignificant problems? Or is he angry for something worse? Is it for something that *I did?* If Sally picks the first one, angry over simple mistakes, she may copy her father by having temper tantrums over minor problems. If she picks the second done—it's my fault—Sally walks on egg-shells in fear of upsetting her father. She also criticizes herself for being so awful, insensitive, and plain stupid for ruining her father's life. Kids who are self-blamers may spiral into a labyrinth of odd thoughts. Thoughts about what *to do* and what *not to do* to prevent her father Marcus' anger.

Controlling Your Anger and Urges

Urges are deadly weapons against patience. Just saying to yourself, "c'mon, calm down" is lame. It doesn't work. Common sense may sound good but is a poor first-aid kit. Later that day or evening, in hindsight, it is easier to review what you *could have done or should have done.* The goal, then, is to prepare yourself ahead of time with as much ammunition of self-control. Let's walk through different strategies that go beyond common sense for better urge control. First is the *Stop–Look–Lower* approach. Second is calming down your body with easy–to–use relaxation steps.

Stop–Look–Lower

Anger follows along a continuum of threshold and then peak until it finally cools down. You can prevent or interrupt your anger by looking carefully at events going on and what can be done to rearrange them. That is what *Stop* is all about. "Stop" right in your tracks as you feel muscular tension and flush sensations racing up and down your spine. Look around at exactly where you are, what is going on, and time schedules. Ask these questions:

1. Am I under a time limit?
2. Am I at a loss for options?
3. Am I upset because I think I can't do this?
4. Is what I want to do being interrupted?
5. Do I want something I can't get?
6. Am I doing two or more things simultaneously?
7. Are there too many obstacles in the way?
8. Am I reading too much into this unpleasant situation?

Answers of "yes" to each item mean urges exist and are disrupting your concentration, especially around family members. The next step after awareness of urges, is to *look*; look around for ways to change these restraints and free yourself of urge traps. For instance, is there any way of giving yourself more time? Or, can you drop the compulsive need for something else? This would eliminate the need to navigate around impossible obstacles. You can gain a new lease on life by identifying as many ways as possible to remove the eight problems shown above.

Jackie's father, Bruce, felt his insides fuming over the spilled milk. He was on the verge of explosion when he *stopped* and *looked.* Here is what he quickly discovered:

1. *Am I under a time limit?* Yes. I must leave for work within 5 minutes and drive Jackie to daycare first before driving in the snow another 5 miles to work.

2. *Am I at a lost for options?* Yes. Darn milk spilled on my tie but I can't figure out another tie that matches with this outfit.

3. *Am I upset because I think I can't do this?* Yes. Matching clothing is not my specialty. Usually I check out outfits with my wife the night before and now my wife is at work. Choosing this tie right now is something new for me.

4. *Is what I want to do being interrupted?* Yes. That milk spilling delays you from taking off with little time to spare.

5. *Do I want something I can't get?* Yes. Ideally I'd like to be on the road heading to work in this lousy weather but the more I rush the farther behind I get at this goal.

6. *Am I doing two or more things simultaneously?* Yes. I was reading the paper, correcting Jackie's homework, and carrying on a conversation with her. All together these activities probably overlooked her need for me to pour the milk in her cereal.

7. *Are there too many obstacles in the way?* Yes. Choosing the tie creates obstacle number one of not knowing which tie. Cleaning the table is obstacle number two. And the lousy snowy weather is obstacle number three.

8. *Am I reading too much into this unpleasant situation?* Yes. I assumed Jackie's spilled her milk for being in a hurry or because she was sloppy.

Alert to his mistakes, now Bruce can *lower* his anger by trying out new alternatives that change the complexion of these conditions. Changes he puts immediately into practice include the following:

1. *Am I under a time limit?* Yes. And I can change this by calling up her daycare or my office and saying I'll be a bit late due to the weather and small accident with the

spilled milk.

2. *Am I at a lost for options?* Yes. But I can change this by creating new options such as asking Jackie to help clean up, while I change my tie.

3. *Am I upset because I think I can't do this?* Yes. But I can change this by picking out a tie myself regardless of what people or my wife might think.

4. *Is what I want to do being interrupted?* Yes. But I can change this by allowing for more time and expecting more interruptions along the way. Interruptions are accidental, not deliberate, and usually occur when doing new or foreign behaviors or are up against unexpected challenges such as the snowy weather.

5. *Do I want something I can't get?* Yes. But I can change this by slowing my pace down and realizing more time is needed to get what I want in smaller steps.

6. *Am I doing two or more things simultaneously?* Yes. I now need to do one task at a time. When I dabble in several tasks simultaneously I must stop for a moment, pay attention to what's going on, and then return to the task.

7. *Are there too many obstacles in the way?* Yes. But each obstacle is only troublesome when I rush. Slowing down the pace allows for concentration and less errors.

8. *Am I reading too much into this unpleasant situation?* Yes. I need to check out my facts by asking Jackie what happened, or putting two and two together including how I was at fault. Blaming Jackie only reverses my anger onto her and makes me feel momentarily better. Whereas ownership of at least some blame forces my awareness of the true facts and steps toward correction.

Relaxation

Popular remedies for relaxation crowd bookstore shelves. Is relaxation achieved through pure imagery? Will visualizing a beach scene in the middle of a department store while your son is screaming at the top of his lungs *really* soothe the spirit? Probably not. How about through acupuncture or medications? Will prescribed sedatives or tranquilizers calm your nerves when Samantha spits up her asparagus on your freshly cleaned floor? Or, when your spouse admits overspending of credit cards when you were out of the country for 5 years? For a moment, maybe. But that's it. Medicine for urge control is not the choice.

PTSD survivors who rely on medicines are kidding themselves. Fast–acting relaxants such as Valium™, Xanax™, Buspar™, Ativan™, among others, are for another purpose. Their compounds distinctly help lower severe anxiety attacks and out of control fears brought on by much more than unwanted stressors. Taking these pills slows your pace down all right, but it also causes side–effects such as drowsiness, disorientation, and sometimes interferes with coordination. Worst of all, relying on medicines as urge controllers gets you into the *habit*. One pill a day doesn't keep the doctor away—it brings you to the doctor more and more for prescription refills because you can't get along without the medicines. Dependency on pills is scary, especially when stressors get you all worked up and there are no pills around. What do you do?

You freak out, literally. Tolerance to medicines forces higher doses and frequent refills to keep you at a balanced state. If popping a pill is your habit under stress, absence of pills will put you in greater excitable fear and paralyze your coping mechanisms with family stress. Withdrawal symptoms, emotionally, include anger, irritability, and intolerance. Add up these symptoms along with not knowing how to manage your family life and the sum total is more severe anxiety than you started off with before taking the medicine.

In other words, think twice, and three times before resorting to drugs for relaxation. A better start is to focus on your muscles. There are muscles that tense up or painfully hurt during urge episodes as you enter threshold and later peak stages. Painful muscular discomfort happens in different spots around your body and you can release this tension following basic steps no matter where you are.

Steps include:
Step 1. Locate the Tension.
Step 2. Intensify and De–intensify.

Step 1. Locate the Tension

Where is it? Where is the tension coming from? This is the first step to relaxation. Most people say tension is felt in the back, neck, thighs, stomach, or wherever there is contact with furniture, clothing or activity. For instance, backache is tension from sitting all day in hard chairs. Foot pain comes from wearing small shoes. Eye-strain from eye fatigue after staring all day at the jiggling black and white computer screen. And so forth.

But tension forms around more than one critical part of the body. Stiffness, muscle spasms or general discomfort can be described on three regions. The first region of muscles includes the head, face, forehead, eyes, mouth, cheekbones, and neck. The second or "middle" region covers the stomach, shoulders, arms, wrists and fingers. A third region includes thighs, legs, feet and toes.

Finding tension among these regions is simple. It doesn't require medical knowledge. Rather, look at yourself and verbally name each of the three muscle areas. At the sound of your voice, assign a number between "0" and "10" to show how much tension is felt. A "0" indicates no tension and "10" indicates much stiffness and tightness.

Now put yourself through a short test. Deliberately stay in tune with your body's muscles while watching, but not acting upon your child's disruptive behavior. Sit there for a moment during a tantrum episode or after he refuses to pick up his clothes. Say nothing for the moment. To yourself record the number (0 to 10) best describing the discomfort you feel. All "10's?" Identify exactly where the "10's" are located. In the first region, second region, or third region? What part of the body?

Frequent muscle restriction, for instance, happens in the first and second regions. In the first region are tight forehead, clenching your teeth, and tight back of neck. In the second region are tight chest, shoulder stiffness, and abdominal tightness. Feel discomfort in any one of these areas? If you do, move rapidly to step 2.

Step 2. Intensify and De–Intensify

Pressure build–up is usually a familiar sensation. Most people know when their body feels in stitches. However, to tell the difference between tension and no tension, attention has to be paid to what muscles feel like when tension goes away. An exercise teaching this sensation to you involves the step of *intensify and de–intensify.*

Intensify is intentionally adding more tension to the known discomfort. It sounds funny, but is very true. Pile more pressure upon the constricted muscle zone by flexing it a bit. Added tension sends a clear message to your body on how hurtful pressure feels. Since sensations vary among muscles, intensifying also familiarizes you with how different muscle groups react under stress.

De–intensify is the favorite part. Release the tightness like a balloon popping. Just let go. All the pressure built up in the intensify part vanishes instantly. It's gone. De–intensify is eliminating pressure so that you can feel the naturally relaxing sensations for a moment or two. Let that free–flowing sensation continue until the muscle begins feeling prickly or "asleep," as when your foot falls asleep. Resist temptation to shake off that sensation or engage in motion to prevent it. As tingling sensations begin, let your hands gently rest on whatever objects are around you. If sitting, place your hands gently on the seat cushion. If standing, lay them gently by your side.

The sequence of intensify to de–intensify goes like this:

INTENSIFY MUSCLES--->WAIT 3 to 5 seconds——>
DE–INTENSIFY MUSCLES

It's helpful to repeat the intensify and de–intensify steps twice on each muscle identified as feeling tight. In fact, practice this exercise at first in private. In bed before getting up in the morning, try out these steps by tightening and loosening problem muscles in each of the three regions. Verbally say to yourself, "tighten, hold, and now loosen."

Effectively using this technique every time urges arise can block that urge from accelerating to the threshold and peak. Control is possible, in other words, but it depends on your deliberate energy to apply this approach. And that's only the beginning.

Returning soldiers who use relaxation agree there is one problem with it. "Will I always have time to use it?" They think intensify and de–intensify steps are too time-consuming. That it involves lying down, working through every muscle, and achieving perfect Karma. Well, not so. It's hard enough stealing a free moment of personal time away from child rearing, let alone a half hour or so for relaxation. That's why relaxation does not require removal of the stressor. *Don't leave the hectic situation. Stay right there.* Use relaxation steps as you feel pressure building directly in the middle of coping with problems. Here is how relaxation fits in these different places.

At home. Miserably rising anger can be countered by stop–look–lower method plus sitting down in a chair or couch. Go through each of the pressured muscles until the tension is gone. Then re–enter the situation using proper methods to handle the situation.

At stores. Rising anger can be countered first, by locating a less busy spot in the store. If using a shopping cart, lean on it with your hands and arms and go through relaxation steps. Next, loosen other bothersome muscular regions before moving the cart. Move the cart forward only when you are ready to press onward. If there is no place to "hide," go into an aisle, pick up a product from the shelf, and concentrate on it while leaning on the cart and undergoing relaxation steps.

At grandma/grandpa's home. This is tougher. There's no doubt about it. At least in stores you can remain anonymous. Here, the audience knows who you are, and what's bothering you. If it is your parents' home, treat it like your own home by locating a chair or couch and begin the exercises. Refuse to explain or defend your actions during relaxation despite persistent inquiries from your parents. And believe me, they will inquire feverishly. Once basic muscles are calmer, return to the difficult situation.

At relatives' homes. Apologies seem greater when the stakes are higher. Here the people are close, but not close enough to be ignored. Again locate that chair or couch, and then ask if one of the adults (or spouse) can watch the misbehaving child for a few minutes. After muscular relief, return to the situation.

At friends' homes. Oddly, risk–taking is easier here because friends probably already know your struggles, fears, and new approaches. Repeat the same approach as you did at a relative's house. Ask your friend to baby–sit for a couple of minutes while you seek refuge on a coach or chair and intensify, then de–intensify muscles.

At a restaurant. Humiliation was meant for restaurants. If another adult is at the table, physically remove the troublemaker (gently) to the lobby, private area, or outside to the car, weather permitting. If your child is the same gender as you, remove yourself and child to the bathroom. Once there, let child just wander a moment while you loosen discomfort and regain control over urges. This is about the only place where leaving the situation for a moment is appropriate. It's obvious why. Certainly your embarrassment is greater, but more problematic is the disruption caused to other people who came to the restaurant for a peaceful meal.

At daycare or school. Just the opposite is true here. Exposure of your child's misbehavior in school is perfectly normal while you calm yourself down. She is around a teacher, peers, and environment that sees the child every day. And hardly every day is a happy day. Again, ask the teacher to watch your son or daughter for a moment while you regain strength through relaxation. Then re–enter the situation.

At scouts, brownies or peer activities. Much like at daycare or school, your child is around peers and other adults. Rising urges can be subdued by excusing yourself for a moment, while your child stays with another adult. Locate that infamous chair or couch and restore muscular comfort.

Anger is Not Control

Anger is not control. Please don't confuse this. Because it's easy to think one means the other. Deterioration of patience may turn into anger as a way of cooling down the situation. And you may really think anger defuses a bad situation. Here is why you think it works: Yelling, screaming, even hitting seems effective because urges immediately disappear once you get angry. No more pain, no more anxiety, no more stress. Your anger felt like you relieved your anxiety and controlled the situation. But this is an illusion. Your anger really did not control anything. You just made the situation worse.

Urges accelerate adult tempers, and it's nothing to be proud of.

Nobody is proud of losing patience or disgracefully having a shouting match with their spouse or children. It feels wrong. You'll see your children or spouse be afraid, stay away from you, or talk back defiantly. Yet, are adult tempers all that bad?

Not always. When anger accidentally leaks out of the emotional bag, it is not immediate cause for alarm. Mistakes do happen in life; and anger mistakes are the most common. Anger is as normal as feeling afraid or unhappy. Overly monitoring your actions to prevent anger is futile. Anger slips out regardless of your best intentions, because urges strike at odd times and are not always preventable and controllable. Last time you suffered the flu was a good example. You got a flu-shot. You even received other immunizations against viral diseases. But the flu virus showed no mercy. It penetrated through your system nonetheless. Remember how you felt? Lousy, irritable, agitated. You tried to remain sweet and fluffy, but that lasted a day. Mildly loud sounds triggered a headache that rang in your ears for days. Physical effort of any sort seemed exhausting. And nothing, no matter how productive your days were, seemed to go right. Illness destroyed your patience and put you at the mercy of your urges.

So, plan on suffering urges. Plan on losing your patience. And, plan on doing the wrong things when you know the right things to do. The difference, though, is plan on making these mistakes less often. And when you make the mistakes, such as having urges, know the rapid ways to recover after an urge-attack.

Never Take It Personally

Walking around on eggshells is awful. You feel nervous, wired, and tuned into every word or gesture people make around you. You feel plugged into everybody's thoughts. You feel plugged into every sound, every noise around you. You're radar is on. And you scan everything you think people say or do. You scan every movement they make, and the movements you think people are going to make. What they're thinking, what they're looking at, and why they're looking at it. It's all buzzing in your mind. It's like a loud radio. Sometimes you can turn it off when you're tired, angry, or laughing. Sometimes it just goes away on its own. But that's rare. You are not paranoid, just scared. You're on watch all of the time.

You see, *you can't afford to turn the scanner off because it is your only way to prevent feeling afraid. You want to catch something before you get caught. Never be caught off guard.* This mindset evolved overseas and possibly before you enlisted in the military. But since you returned from duty, you've noticed how much more you're hyperalert to the world. This is called *hypervigilance.*

Hypervigilance occurs for two main reasons: To avoid surprises and eliminate fear. Fear-elimination by being extra-alert to people around you allows you to anticipate conflicts, criticisms, and any problems making you feel inferior. Constant awareness keeps you on your toes. You're always on guard. The more you see, the more you hear, the more you know—the better you're prepared. You'll get them before they get you. You're anxiety alarm is always on-call, ready to be turned on at a moment's notice and your entire personality sets into self-defense.

Do you know why this happens? It's because you feel that anything you do naturally is wrong. That is a major symptom of PTSD. The paralyzing fear that you cannot do anything right. Or that no matter what you do, something bad will still happen. You doubt everything you do naturally. Everything is suspicious. Talking naturally seems wrong. Smiling naturally is wrong. Walking naturally is wrong. You don't *think* it's wrong, *it is* wrong. And so you anticipate people around you also perceive it as wrong. You're waiting for their disapproval by sizing up the situation and mentally calculating how and why people perceive your action as wrong. This mental calculus goes on in great detail. It gets obsessive. It's more complex than a computer. In your mind you figure out several things all at once without anybody knowing it. It's not just "what are they thinking?" it's more like:

1. Why is she angry?
2. She only gets angry when such and such happens.
3. Did I do such and such?
4. I must have, and here's how it happened.
5. I could have done it this way—yah, that would have been better.
6. Okay, what are the consequences for what I did?
7. What are the chances this bad thing will happen today, maybe tomorrow?
8. After it happens, what then? I don't know. I better run through that scenario in my mind.

Its' a game of logic inside your brain. Deduction after deduction. Speculation after speculation. It goes on and on and on. You work up a sweat from your mental gymnastics by probing every possible angle the situation may go in. You graphically imagine the situation through catastrophic scenarios. You're staging the whole performance from start to finish—deciding who say things, when they will say it, and how you will respond to it. You're director, choreographer, and audience all in one. It all runs smoothly through your mental circuitry until there's a snag. Snags you can't figure out start a panic. "Oh my God, what am I going to do?" You re-run the scenarios, switch the dialogue, redo the action, and play it out again until it *feels right. Until it feels like you absolutely can prevent conflict and feel shame.*

The mind-games you go through are stressful. You work so hard internally at strategizing a win-win situation that you lose touch with life. Life seems awful because it's like a chess match. Every move takes twenty minutes to figure out. You concentrate on concentrating. Will it always be that slow? Or, can I ever go faster?

Yes, you can go faster. That's what this chapter is going to teach you. This is where you learn how you read into things and how to stop doing it.

How You Read Into Things

You read into people's actions by intuition. No, you're not psychic, although you probably feel you are. Yes, you've predicted things before. Yes, you sense things in the world that other people are completely oblivious to. And yes, you're like a thermometer. You always know when people will reach their boiling points. And why shouldn't you know this? Growing up as a child or in adulthood you watched anything and everything that happened around you so that you didn't get in trouble. The more you tuned into life, the more control you felt. So, here's what you've done instinctively for a long time:

1. You watch and listen to people very closely. The more important they are to you, the closer you zero-in on them.
2. You say to yourself, "She's doing that because of why she's done that before." Whatever reason in the past accounted for her action is the reason you think she's doing it now.

3. You say to yourself, "Why would I do what she's doing?" Whatever reason you might have for doing what this person is doing, becomes her reason for doing it.

4. You say to yourself, "Is there somebody at fault here?" Sure there is. *There's always somebody at fault when you think, eat and breathe guilt.* You blame either yourself or the other person. If it's her fault, then you think "She should have, could have done something differently" or "She always does this bad thing to me." If you blame yourself, then you think "I should have, could have done something to prevent this conflict—*God am I stupid.*"

Let's look again at all four steps in reading into things:

- watch behavior
- assume they're doing it because of what they did in the past.
- assume they're doing it because of why you'd do it to them.
- assume they're to blame or that you're the one at fault.

You're assuming too much. Assumptions start from CSWs or COULD BEs, SHOULD BEs and WOULD BEs. They're not based in facts. Facts are skipped over because you think you have all the answers. You feel compelled your reasons are truth. They feel true, *so they must be true.*

How to Stop Reading Into Things

Can you stop the roller coaster ride before you get nauseous? Does it just go up and down forever? It has thus far and probably will keep going until push the STOP button. So, here's where to push the button.

You can prevent assumptions by taking simple steps as you read them on paper. Of course, nothing is *really* simple about them. They only sound simple because the steps will make logical sense. And you're a whiz at logic. But when you know *what to do* and *how to do it*, fears about trying the steps will go away.

Basic Steps to Prevent Assumptions

Only genies can look through crystal balls and foresee the future. But you can predict the future without a crystal ball by just sensing mischief is around the corner. Of course, you're just guessing. Guesswork is loaded with assumptions piled high over time from trying to know everything and being certain about nothing. You can interrupt the flow of assumptions by following five steps:

Step 1. Look at only "what" the person is saying and doing, not "why" he is saying or doing it.

Try this experiment for starters. Look up at somebody around you right now. Watch their body motions. Now describe exactly what you see. Is he making faces? Is he moving his hands a lot? Describe physical movements in dry and simple terms. Such as, "He's laughing," "he's walking fast," "he's talking fast," and "he's looking at a book." The more concrete you describe it, the better the description is.

Now the verbal end of things. Try listening to what the person around you is saying to somebody else. Again, describe this action in very plain language. For example, "She's talking about shoes," "she's telling the other person about what her mother did." *Why* this person is saying these things *is unimportant. Stick only with what is going on, not why. Don't read into it, under it, over it, or anything else about it except what you see or hear. Cut your other senses off from making judgments.*

Step 2: Think questions about what, not why.

At first you have to shift gears. You're so used to reading into *why* things happen that ignoring the *why* seems wrong. But it isn't wrong. You're only feeling it's wrong because you're doing something new. And new things never feel right.

Now describe the same action you did a moment ago, but this time put a "WHY?" in front of it. Ask a question as if you were speaking to the person nearby. You'd ask, "Why are you laughing?," "Why are you walking fast?" "Why are you talking about your shoes?," "Why are you telling another person about your mother?" Questions pointedly check out your facts.

Step 3: No facts, No fault (F&F).

You're going to ask people questions because you don't know exactly why something is happening. And when you don't know *the facts*, don't blame yourself. That's called *F & F* ; or "no facts, no fault." If you don't have the facts, it's not your fault. You see, when somebody says or does something to you, ask yourself these questions and answer them a new way:

1. What am I assuming here? You're assuming you did something wrong.
- NEW ANSWER: I don't know what's going on here because I don't have the facts. And, no facts, no fault—F & F.

2. Why is the assumption wrong? It's wrong because you lack facts.
- NEW ANSWER: Again, If I don't have the facts, it's not my fault—F & F.

3. Why am I bad person? You're assuming you're bad because the person is talking to you and something *may be wrong.*
- NEW ANSWER: You're never bad. You're just not sure. It's okay to be unsure. Check out your facts.

4. Why am I better than others? I couldn't possibly be better. I'm scum.
- NEW ANSWER: I'd never do what this person is doing right now. I am better than this person at this moment in time.

5. What should I do instead of feel scared? Nothing, be nice and run away.
- NEW ANSWER: Ask a question about what is going on, not why it is happening

Step 4.Ask Questions directly

Okay, here you go. First chance you get, ask a significant other why he or she says or does something. Right now, go into your son, daughter, spouse or intimate's room and ask "Why did you say that to me a moment ago?" Spit the words out. If it was what he did, not said to you, say "Why did you do that to me?" Phrase your question so that you ask about what you saw or heard. Be careful not to answer the question when you ask it. That happens when you ask, "Why are you angry at me?"

But do you know if the person is angry at you? Really? *No, you don't know and you're not going to invite the person to say he or she is angry at you. Give no opportunities for people to blame you.* Just ask the question in a straight-forward way: "Why did you do that?," or "Why did you say that?"

Step 5: Resist anxiety relief

You did it. You actually got the question out of your mouth. Okay, take a breather. That's one giant step for mankind. Now, stay where you are. Don't move, don't go backwards. It's not the end of the world. And for heavens sake, *don't be fooled by your inner messages.* Your body is sending you distress signals warning you to "abort operation" and make amends before things get out of hand. You're itching to say, "Look, I'm sorry for asking you that silly question. Please forgive me." You feel the words form in your throat. Now they're on the tip of your tongue—HOLD IT.

Don't say "You're sorry." Don't say you're sorry because you're not sorry. You did nothing wrong. *No facts, no fault—F & F.* You must resist the rising anxiety that scares you into your old habits. Anxiety is when your body gets tense, you feel your thoughts spinning, your hands get sweaty, and all you hear yourself repeat is OH GOD, AM I IN DEEP SH—.

No you're not. You can resist old habits by not relieving anxiety. It's okay to be anxious a little bit. That's normal. It doesn't mean you'll faint. Stay alert. Here are the wrong things to do. Don't do these things and you won't get more nervous:

DON'T:
say your sorry
defend yourself
start complimenting the other person
put yourself down

excuses
blaming somebody else
cry
do something nice for other person
laugh nervously
change the subject
remain silent

There is nothing shameful about asking questions. Questions feel strange because you're afraid the person will tell you precisely what you fear—that you really are a bad person. But better you learn the facts first, than to conjure them up on your own. You will always distort the details if you make assumptions.

Roadblocks to look out for

You've taken the plunge off the cliff and never thought you'd make it safely to the bottom. Well, you have. You can ask questions about the way things are, not how you think they are. You can block automatic assumptions before they tongue-tie you into fear. This makes you feel stronger, more in control, and more spontaneous.

Questions at first feel funny but than you get over their strangeness. Other people, however, may take longer to get used to your questions. Think for a moment: How long have you been making assumptions? You're whole life? That means people who live with you know you by your habits. They are accustomed to you tiptoeing around them, feeling guilty all the time, and *especially,* not asking them questions. They would flip if you asked them a question. They wouldn't know how to react and what to say. So, they say what naturally enters their mind—and usually it's not very nice.

First time reactions to your questions can be negative. "What did you say to me?" or "Who do you think you're talking to?" raise the lid on your escape hatch, ready for ejection. You hate thinking you caused somebody grief and this is precisely what you may have done. Right?

Not exactly. You did catch the person off guard. They're not sure which way to go—left, right or right down the center. So they punt. One way is by throwing you for a loop with nasty remarks, called

48

roadblocks. Roadblocks are not intentional. Few people actually stay up nights to rehearse undermining tactics. It just comes naturally as a defense against looking stupid. You're questions instantly put the person on the defensive because he lacks a response. You've never done this before and so he never needed to respond to you before. Now he does and he doesn't know what to do.

Several roadblocks fly through the air as attempts to restore a comfort zone. Comfort zones for other people are having you be your polite, guilty self again. People want you to drop your courage, get on your knees, and beg for forgiveness; then, they'll stop throwing roadblocks. But you have no intentions on going backwards. It was a long haul getting you this far and you're on a hot streak now. No turning back. That means bulldozing through roadblocks by handling them the right way. So, get used to hearing the following remarks said to you after you ask questions and replying to them a certain way:

1. ROADBLOCK:"Why are you asking me that question, Don't ask me that!"
- ANSWER:"I'm just wondering."

2. ROADBLOCK:"You wonder too much. Keep your thoughts to yourself."
- ANSWER:"I'm sorry you feel that way"

When people get all huffy about your questions, use the conventional reply, "I'm just wondering" or "I'm sorry you feel that way." It instantly defuses defensive anger and makes the person feel silly for being rude. You, on the other hand, remain calm and collected. Take a breath, relax, and look at who is really getting nervous. It's not you—it's the other person. That person is so dizzy from your unexpected question that her remarks are running in circles. Nothing makes sense to her. That person lost control for a moment. And you picked up control where you never found it before—right in the palm of your hands.

You're in charge, but a larger battalion of roadblocks is on its way. Roadblocks get nastier if the person literally has been verbally or physically abusive to you in the past. The person who always criticizes you, hits you, or has an emotional or substance abuse problem will get rougher in spite of your civil remarks. Their roadblocks get more interesting but are treated the same way. Here some common examples with ways to react to the roadblocks.

1. ROADBLOCK:"There you go sticking your nose in other people's business."
    - *Why they say it:* Person is turning the topic around on you to avoid feeling stupid.
    - ANSWER:That's not the point. I was just wondering.

2. ROADBLOCK:"You're never satisfied with anything I do—God your awful."
    - *Why they say it:*Person is re-interpreting the topic and going way beyond the key points.
    - ANSWER:I'm sorry you feel that way. But I was just wondering.

3. ROADBLOCK:"Listen, damn it, you ask me one more damn time and I'll show you whose boss here."
    - *Why they say it:*Person is threatening you with physical harm knowing that in the past this would "shut you up" immediately.
    - ANSWER"I'm sorry you feel that way. I'm just wondering."

4. ROADBLOCK:"Boy do you look cute when you're pissed"
    - *Why they say it:*Belittling you with humor eases the person's tension.
    - ANSWER"That's not the point. The point is (repeat your question)."

5. ROADBLOCK:"God, did I hurt your feelings? I'm such a horrible person. Don't look at me, I'm so stupid. "
    - *Why they say it:*Self-demeaning remarks in the past draw your sympathy.
    - ANSWER"I'm sorry you feel that way." (Repeat your question).

6. ROADBLOCK:(Yelling loudly) "Shut the F— up. "

- *Why they say it:*Aggressively loud threats in the past stopped you dead in your tracks. The person is hoping it will do the same thing again.
- ANSWER:"I'm just wondering." (Repeat your question.)

7. ROADBLOCK:"You just keep this up, you lousy skunk, and I'll tell the kids (or your family) what a jerk you really are."

- *Why they say it:*Person threatens to expose your "weak" side hoping your need for approval will stop your questions.
- ANSWER:"I'm sorry you feel that way." (Repeat question.)

Roadblocks missiled toward your soft ego are tie-breakers. If the score is even, and you're holding up but feeling nervous, you may collapse under tough criticisms. The more "personal" criticisms are, the more you feel compelled to react defensively. "How dare that person insult me that way!" But don't do that. Defensiveness gets you off track. You lose the link between *F & F* and asking questions. You'd plummet backwards into old habits while the other person breathes a sigh of relief for escaping an uncomfortable situation. And that's precisely what you don't want to happen. You *do want that person to experience discomfort until he or she realizes you're really serious and won't give up.*

Reversal of Guilt

Does that mean all roadblocks are off-limits? No, not exactly. One roadblock that is healthy is reversing guilt. You reverse guilt by asking questions when you're:

1. Not sure why the person is asking or telling you something
2. About to be accused of something you did or didn't do
3. Out of facts and need more facts before replying intelligibly

Questions transfer the weight of shame from your shoulders to the other person's shoulders long enough to hear more facts on what's going on. Replies they give you when you reverse guilt are surprising. You may learn *it's not your fault after-all.* Or, *something else is going on completely unexpected.* For example, Cheryl heard her husband in the garage swearing up a storm and throwing his tools. She automatically assumed she misplaced his tools. But she reversed this guilt by going into the garage and asking him for facts: "Why are you yelling?" He replied that his brother borrowed his tool yesterday and forgot to return it. He also admitted the fact that he was tired and felt a cold coming on. Cheryl discovered: *It had nothing to do with Cheryl.*

By reversing the burden of shame, you force a person to explain what's going on in the situation. You can resist blaming yourself for things you didn't do but think you did. You can resist rescuing the situation from conflict and making the person feel like a happy camper. You don't step in and hurt yourself or repair anything because you *won't do that without your facts.* You're facts are the life-blood of your social interaction. Think only facts. Look only at facts. Talk only facts. And suspend the verdict of guilty toward yourself or other people until all the facts are lined up in a neat order for you to discuss aloud.

Other Ways to Overcome PTSD

Post-traumatic Reversal Methods

E motional survivors of PTSD can be gullible. Like terminally-ill patients, they may settle for unproved therapy knowing that rumors attest to its benefits. Rumors may promise the miracle of complete symptom relief; but no real therapy can do that. Rumors start from faith, prayer, and even placebo effects. Thinking it works can be an illusion. But that illusion may cure you. Deeply believing a therapy works is why many offbeat methods are attractive. Such methods promise less effort, emotional purification, and life-renewal. That's why many avante garde therapies using Eastern and Western ways become popular.

PTSD trauma is erased only partially when emotions are purified and life is restored. It also involves regaining key losses you suffered during the repeated war-trauma. Losses subjugate your mind. You feel worthless and afraid. And you want the "you" back the way you were before the traumatic experience. Alternative therapies may try restoring these losses but scientific therapies can definitely recapture them.

The six losses you experienced and can be returned include *safety, purpose, power, validity, hope,* and *dignity.*

- *Safety is knowing you can protect yourself.*
- *Purpose is knowing you have an identity and meaning in life and what life holds for you.*
- *Power is being in control and having a sense of destiny.*
- *Validity is certainty of your life experiences and feeling anchored in reality.*
- *Hope is more than faith; it is optimism for a healthy peaceful world you can survive in.*
- *Dignity is respect. You take comfort knowing human beings are unconditionally caring.*

Losses do not recover automatically. They do not regenerate like skin tissue. Personal and calculated effort goes into repairing a loss until you feel the emptiness gone and your emotions filled with inspiration. To reach this point, consider three solidly tested therapies used with PTSD survivors. Therapies include *desensitization, thought-feeling therapy (TFT), Eye Movement Desensitization and Reprocessing (EMDR).*

Desensitization. Desensitization is a series of careful steps where you self-teach control over fear. Fear, remember, is a biological and emotional state. Thoughts you hear inside your mind trigger cardiovascular, abdominal and other involuntary muscles to constrict making you feel discomfort. As constriction occurs, the hormone adrenaline pumps feverishly throughout your body, sending waves of electrical current up and down your spine. While hot-wired inwardly, your outer self is pairing fear with the places, people and settings encountered. Jolts of fear in your car turn your car into a phobic place. Fear associated with late evenings or dark skies transforms the outdoors into anxious objects. You want nothing to do with them.

So, you avoid them like the plague. Overwhelming fear can reduce you world into a claustrophobic trap. Many times, uncured anxiety sufferers become so afraid, they hate to travel outside their homes, a disorder called agoraphobia. But a simple anxiety-defusal method can prevent anxiety from overtaking your life. Here is how you can use desensitization. Just follow these easy steps:

1. Identify which people and situations cause fear. Construct a list from strong fears to weak fears. Rank your order based on a scale of 1 to 10. Assign a "1" to weak fears and "10" to strong fears.

2. Choose a strong fear. Picture it vividly in your mind. As you feel your body swivel and a chill rushes up your spine, immediately picture yourself doing the one thing you find peacefully relaxing. For example, resting on empty beach away from the threat of abductors and entirely safe from intrusion--doesn't that feel nice? Guide your body to a calming, composed state by tightening and loosening cramped muscles. With your toes, for example, pinch them inward tightly; then let go. With your wrists, bend them inward and make a fist; now let go. Tighten any muscle or body part feeling anxious. Then release the tension just as quickly.

3. Now savor in that sensually relaxed feeling for 1-2 minutes. Permit no distractions as you engage in this image.

4. Repeat steps #1 through #3 for fear objects you ranked 6 and higher. Do this for one week.

5. Now look for an actual picture, line drawing or figurine resembling the fearful objects pictured in your mind. With a modest fearful object first, look at it within a distance of 1-2 feet. Look right through it as if it were transparent. See, you're not afraid of it anymore, are you? No. As you feel tension build, imagine that wonderful beach scene and feeling relaxed. Tighten and loosen muscles where you feel tingling. But, keep your eyes peeled to that fearful object. As your body feels okay with that object,

go to the next higher ranked object of fear and repeat this step over again. Keep doing the steps until you feel no anxiety around the strongest fearful object.

6.   Finally, take a quantum leap beyond objects to anything faintly reminding you that fear. Conversations, books, book covers, pictures--anything picturing an alien or abductor. Test your comfort level by closing in the gap between you and the object. Actually hold the object, wear the object, or engage in conversation. Be part of that object's world, rather than a prisoner of it. Again, pay close attention to your muscle strain. As anxiety rises, quickly tighten and loosen muscles and body parts without aborting contact with the fearful objects.

Thought-feeling therapy (TFT). TFT is a revolutionary new approach using the Eastern art of acupuncture with desensitization. It uses the body's energy system to combat negative emotions such as fear and depression. A simple process of massaging tender pressure points around the body , called algorithms, tempers stress and opens up your mind to redirection. By stimulating these "meridian" points, you not only release blocked emotions such as pain and anger, you also release the thoughts suppressing those emotions.

TFT begins with a basic understanding of sensory points on the body. There are many of them ranging from your head and neck to your toes. Any book on acupuncture will amply guide you through a complete inventory of these meridian points. For now, let's consider the soft, fleshy area centrally located to the immediate left or right of your sternum. Specifically, adjacent to the manubrium. Rub this area from left to right as you re-describe the same picture used in the desensitization exercise above. This time, however, add an additional feature. Tell yourself how confident you are, and that you can overcome any defeat.

Intricately touching and massaging these pressure points coupled with words of inspiration is simple and rapid to do. But be sure you follow the coordinates on the body to pinpoint correct pressure areas.

Eye movement desensitization and reprocessing (EMDR). More than any approach used today, EMDR touts the greatest success for PTSD. It is an innovative clinical treatment that has successfully helped over a million individuals who have survived trauma, including sexual abuse, domestic violence, combat, crime, and those suffering from other complaints including depressions, addictions, phobias and a variety of self-esteem issues. It involves stimulating eye movement in ways that stimulate the brain's information processing systems.

Internal negative messages instantly dissipate while you flicker your eyes back and forth while focusing on painful phobic memories. The process from beginning to end goes like this:

1. Induce saccadic eye movements. This means, rapidly shift your eyes laterally back and forth for one minute. To help activate eye motion, use your hand 12 inches in front of your eyes, lifting one or two fingers across your visual field. As your fingers shift left, follow the fingers with your eyes. Then, watch them as your fingers shift to the right. Gently shift you fingers back and forth like a pendulum, tracking them continuously.

2. As visual tracking occurs, mentally picture the worst part of the trauma. For example, being tied down by captors; or food-deprived for hours. Hold onto this hideous image while laterally shifting your eyes.

3. With the image in tact and eyes rotating, feel your entire body engulfed in panic. Take inventory of your discomfort permeating from top to bottom and allow it to flow freely. Now, abruptly stop the anxiety by taking a deep breath. Stop the mental image. Focus on the left and right movement of the fingers. Concentrate on them. Hypnotically you will feel less anxiety and more entranced in pacing your eyes and face with the shifting fingers.

4.   Repeat this method several times paired with internal mental cues of higher-order fear. Just as before, rank the order of fearful places, persons or objects. Let the highest ranked fear internally flash before your eyes when undergoing this exercise.

A final word about EMDR. Results are still trickling in on its long-term effectiveness. Like any simplified method, risks associated with it are important to consider. One risk is dizziness. Traumatized patients who get dizzy easily or have vestibular imbalance are not advised to use this approach. Low vision or other visual limitations will minimize the power of results as well. Finally, be prepared for resurgence. Symptom relief may be fast and you can feel overconfident of your progress. But like any PTSD, symptoms may resurface unexpectedly and require you to re-apply the same steps over again.

Don't despair. Repeating a good thing is better than having no solution at all.

No cure is infallible. PTSD is a stubborn disorder that can be rekindled accidentally and undermine your confidence. While these therapies block many recurrent symptoms and restore your happiness, they do not entirely inoculate you from flashbacks. For this, you may require a more potent method to fight off the hypnotic-trance induced by fears. Directly combating this loss of control is a two step process called *Assertion and Anger Release*

Assertion and anger release (AAR). Protecting yourself from repeat anxiety-intrusions takes courage and know-how. Courage comes from mustering strength to confront the object of your fear. Know-how is the decisive, methodical effort of being in control from the outset so you are mentally and physically alert. Your goal is simple; replace your vulnerability for abuse by asserting an equal standing with the fear. Prove to yourself, you can resist mental take-over.

The steps for self-control are twofold. First involves *assertion.* Second involves *anger release.*

Assertion involves, first, telling yourself you are not a victim. You are not trapped, controlled or overruled. Fear is what puts you in that state. Second, verbalize every night before going to bed or wherever traumatic memories arise, that you will stay in the situation and prevail, not surrender to internal terror. You will dictate what happens, where you go, and when you go. Reassure yourself of your confidence by rehearsing scripted lines on what you'll say. Practice saying these lines aloud in general or to a trusted person, sympathetic with your ordeal. Third, set your clock to an hour midway through your sleeping cycle. Or practice this midway through whatever activity involves trauma-memory. Awake briefly to reassure yourself you still feel confident. Briefly awakening in the middle of the night or interrupting the activity, gains control over the situation.

Anger release. Anger is real. Inside your body lies a volcano verging on explosion. Annoyed and terrified, you've pondered ways to retaliate against captors or even the power of death. But you cannot figure out how to do it. Anger grows like an infectious disease spreading bitterness and resentment throughout your system. All you can think about is somehow restoring your dignity and destroying the twisted and debilitating effects of trauma.

This passion for self-cure is therapeutic. Three steps let you viably use anger as a weapon against future PTSD episodes of anxiety. First, gather up all signs, symbols, pictures, illustrations and objects resembling the vivid memories of your trauma. Both mentally and aloud, shout out your anger at them. Treat them like a stranger who you caught robbing your house or verbally abusing you. Criticize, ridicule, and discredit the memories for their disrespect, ignoble methods, and invasions of your privacy.

Second, keep score. Every morning you awake untroubled, note it down as a victory. While a private win, you just proved you could patrol and protect yourself from mental intrusion. And why?

Because you are in control and vigilantly monitoring for memory intruders. You will meet this intrusion with resistance and instantly eliminate the bad memories.

Taking a hard-head approach to PTSD effects may seem futile at first, since you view yourself as a victim against holocaust-like experiences. But specie survival is the same along any phylogenetic scale—the tougher you are, the more you survive. The roughest, toughest, and pushiest of the beasts outsmarts the weakest animal. Darwin had it right. Aggression presents a strange and unusual phenomena to combat unwanted thoughts, emotions, and avoidant behaviors. Anger liberates you from inhibition and depression. You fight back, as you were trained to, under duress and especially threatening conditions. PTSD poses ongoing threats to your happiness, and requires your combative posture against it.

Don't be another statistic. PTSD indiscriminately strikes anybody at anytime for the most unsuspecting activity. Not you, though. You are a fighter, a skillfully and methodically trained machine capable of weathering any psychological storm. You will always rise above fears of the unknown and terrors of what you do know. That is why you joined the military: To join this prestigious rank of highly perceptive and self-disciplined people. Individuals packed with fortitude, determination, and resilience. You can bounce back. You can live a post-war life as you did before, and with positive memories of your tours of duty. You have a right to do this, and it depends entirely on your faith in yourself as a teacher and healer.

Trust yourself, and trust your practice of the methods described in this book. Fear, after all, is what we make it. And when you want fear to go away forever, just give the command.